LIFEWAYS

The Inuit

RAYMOND BIAL

BENCHMARK BOOKS

MARSHALL CAVENDISH
NEW YORK

SERIES CONSULTANT: JOHN BIERHORST

ACKNOWLEDGMENTS

The Inuit could not have been written without the kind help of many people and organizations that have devoted themselves to preserving the traditions of the Inuit.

I would like to acknowledge my editors Kate Nunn and Doug Sanders for their many insightful comments on the manuscript. I again thank John Bierhorst for his fine critical review and his knowledgeable help with the stories included in this volume. As always, I offer my deepest thanks for my wife, Linda, and my children, Anna, Sarah, and Luke, for their wonderful inspiration.

Benchmarks Books
Marshall Cavendish Corporation
99 White Plains Road, Tarrytown, New York 10591-9001
Text copyright © 2002 by Raymond Bial
Map copyright © 2002 by the Marshall Cavendish Corporation
Map by Rodica Prato

Library of Congress Cataloging-in-Publication Data
Bial, Raymond.
The Inuit / by Raymond Bial.
p. cm. — (Lifeways)
Includes bibliographical references and index.
ISBN 0-7614-1212-3
1. Inuit—Juvenile literature. 2. Eskimos—Juvenile literature. [1. Inuit. 2. Eskimos.] I. Title.
E99.E7 B49 2001   979.8004'971—dc21   00-052892
Printed in Italy
6 5 4 3 2 1

Photo Research by Candlepants Incorporated

Cover Photo: Wolfgang Kaehler

The photographs in this book are used by permission and through the courtesy of: *Corbis*: Historical Picture Archive, 1, 51; Galen Rowell, 6; Lowell Georgia, 48, 58, 102-103; Wolfgang Kaehler, 8-9, 10, 11, 14, 72,76-77, 98-99, 100-101, 105, 106; Underwood & Underwood, 17; Dan Guravich, 23; David Muench, 25; Corbis, 28-29, 37, 38-39, 67, 80-81, 86, 89; Hulton-Deutsch Collection, 31, 41, 54, 57, 65, 79; Michael Maslan Historical Photographs, 34, 60, 90-91, 96, 111; Bettmann, 36, 95; Museum of History and Industry, 43; PEMCO Webster & Stevens Collection, 45; Staffan Widstrand, 53; Michael Lewis, 68; Peter Harholdt, 74, 83 (top and lower); *Alaska State Library,Early Prints of Alaska Collection #01-652*: 113; *Yousuf Karsh/Woodfin Camp and Associates*:115.

This book is dedicated to the Inuit who have learned to live joyfully in the harshest climate on Earth.

Contents

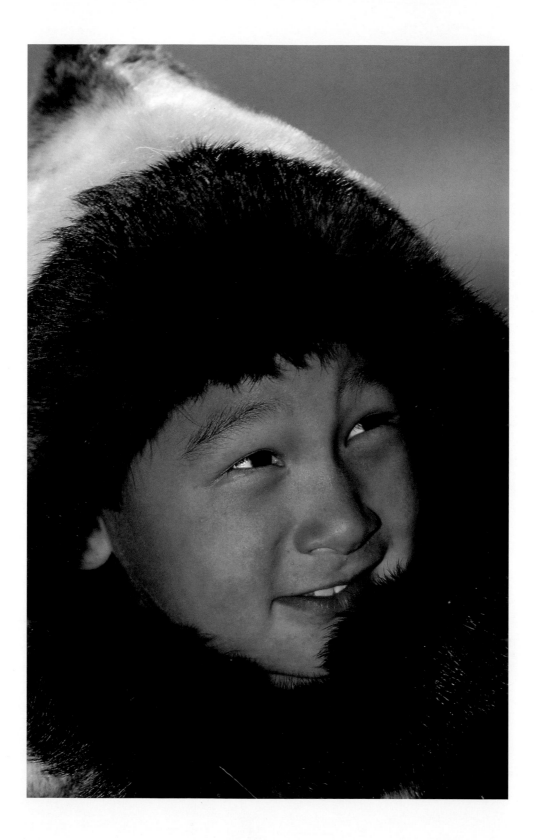

Author's Note

At the dawn of the twentieth century, Native Americans were thought to be a vanishing race. However, despite four hundred years of warfare, deprivation, and disease, American Indians have not gone away. Countless thousands have lost their lives, but over the course of this century the populations of native tribes have grown tremendously. Even as American Indians struggle to adapt to modern Western life, they have also kept the flame of their traditions alive—the language, religion, stories, and the everyday ways of life. An exhilarating renaissance in Native American culture is now sweeping the nation from coast to coast.

The Lifeways books depict the social and cultural life of the major nations, from the early history of native peoples in North America to their present-day struggles for survival and dignity. Historical and contemporary photographs of traditional subjects, as well as period illustrations, are blended throughout each book so that readers may gain a sense of family life in a tipi, a hogan, or a longhouse.

No single book can comprehensively portray the intricate and varied lifeways of an entire tribe, or nation. I only hope that young people will come away with a deeper appreciation for the rich tapestry of Indian culture—both then and now—and a keen desire to learn more about these first Americans.

1.Origins

During the brief arctic summers, the tundra thaws and bursts with life.

ONCE KNOWN AS ESKIMOS, THE INUIT (IN OO IT) HAVE LONG INHABITED the northern reaches of Asia and North America, a vast land of ice and snow stretching from Siberia across Alaska to eastern Canada and Greenland. Here, at the top of the world, the sun follows an unusual seasonal cycle, glowing day and night through the brief months of summer. Through the long winters, the sun sets in mid-November and does not reappear until mid-January. All this while the snow-whitened tundra is mostly covered in darkness. For generations the Inuit have told stories to help them through the light-filled days and the long stretch of seemingly endless nights. Here is a version of one such tale told by Apagkaq, a Mackenzie River Inuit, about the raven and how people came to live in this harsh and challenging environment.

The Creation

He was quite alone on Earth, squatting in the darkness. Suddenly he became conscious and discovered himself, but he had no idea where he was. Nor did he know how he had gotten there. But he breathed, and there was life in him. He lived!

But who was he? A being—something living. Anything beyond that he could not comprehend. All about him was darkness, and he could see nothing.

Then he groped about with his hands. Wherever he touched his fingers brushed over clay. The earth was lifeless clay, as was everything else about him.

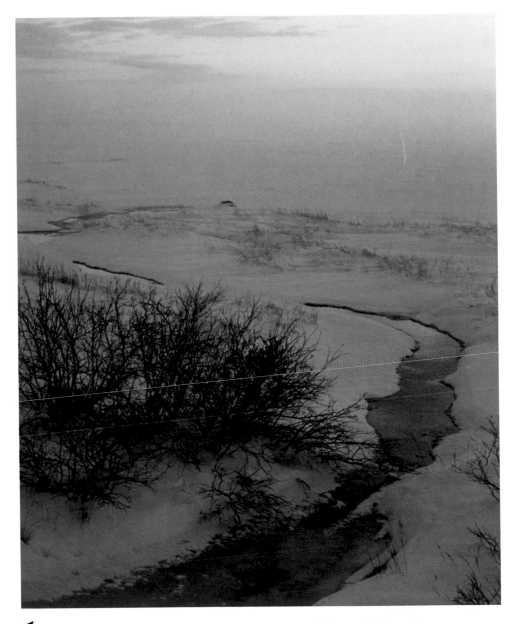

In comparison to our own, the far north is a world out of kilter. The summer days are filled with hours of sunlight, while winter can seem like a string of endless nights.

He let his fingers glide over himself. He knew nothing of how he looked, but he found his face and felt that he had a nose, eyes and mouth, arms and legs and limbs. He was a human being—a man!

He felt his forehead and found a hard little bump. What was that for?

He began to reflect. He understood that he was a separate being. He started to crawl across the clay, slowly and cautiously. He wanted to find out where he was. But suddenly his hands felt only empty space—an abyss—and he dared not go on.

He squatted and wondered how he might discover what the great black darkness held. He broke off a piece of clay and threw it into the abyss. He listened for the clay to reach the bottom, but no sound came back to him.

He moved away from the abyss and found a hard object on the ground. He pushed it into the clay. Why he did so he did not know; he simply did it. Then he sat still again, lost in thought and wondering what was in the darkness.

Suddenly a sound startled him. He heard a flutter in the air, and a small, light thing settled on his hand. With his other hand he touched this mysterious visitor and found that it had a bill, warm soft feathers all over its body, and small naked feet.

It was a little sparrow. All at once he understood that it had been there all along, flying over him and hopping about him in the darkness. He had simply not noticed the sparrow until it landed on his hand.

The man liked the company of the little bird. He felt bolder and crawled over the ground till he came to the object he had stuck into the clay. Then he discovered that it had taken root. A tree grew out of the ground, and soft grass had sprouted on the clay!

He crawled to the tree. Other trees had grown around it, one beside another. They had become a forest. Small plants formed a lush carpet on the forest floor, and he passed his hand over them. He felt their shape and smelled their fragrance. But still he could see nothing.

The man wanted to know more about this strange place, so he crept along with the little sparrow fluttering above his head. He could not see it, but he heard the sound of its wings. He also felt the bird when it settled on his head or hopped onto his hand. The man crawled because he dared not walk blindly through the darkness.

He wanted to know what was in the abyss and asked the sparrow to fly down and explore it. The little bird flew away. It was gone so long that the man thought the sparrow would never return. Finally, the sparrow returned and landed on his head holding a fresh shoot in its bill.

The fresh shoot made the man want to explore the depths of the abyss himself. He asked the sparrow to perch on his knee so he could examine its body to learn how it could fly on its small wings. Groping his way through the forest, the man broke off branches and attached them to his shoulders. As he flapped the branches, they became real wings. Feathers sprouted on his body and the lump on his forehead

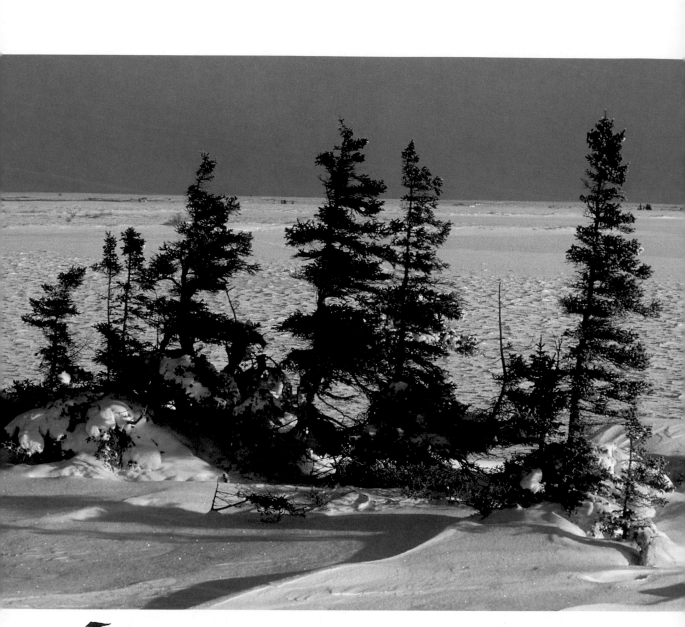

*T*rees are a rare sight in Inuit territory, which is mostly flat or rolling land blanketed with snow.

grew into a bill. Suddenly, he realized that he could fly like the little sparrow.

It was still dark, and he could see nothing. He asked the sparrow to fly in front of him so that he could hear the beating of its wings. As the man left the ground, he cried, "Kowk-kowk." He had turned into a big black bird, and he called himself a raven.

The raven named the place they had left the sky. It was a long way from the sky to the land of the abyss. The raven struggled to keep himself in the air, but he and the sparrow finally arrived at the land of the abyss. The raven planted the land of the abyss in the same manner as he had planted in the sky. Soon there was forest everywhere, and herbs and flowers grew among the trees. This new land the raven called the world.

Then the raven created people. He shaped them of clay. So there might be food for them, he created the animals of the land, air, and sea. He told the people of the world that these animals would sustain them.

In those first days of the world, nothing could be seen. The people had to feel or listen to find their way. The people heard caribou bulls calling in deep throaty tones, wolves howling, bears growling, foxes calling, "kak-kak-kak." From the sea they could hear the snorting of seals, the bellowing of walruses, and the calling of whales, "Puh-puh-puh!" They heard birds screaming and singing. They heard the sighing of the wind in the forests, the rustling and whispering of the leaves, and the crash of the breakers on the shore.

The people were surrounded by life and sound, but still they could see nothing. Everywhere they groped in the darkness. It was hard to catch animals for food. So, the raven called the little sparrow and said, "You were there before I found myself sitting on the ground. Fly out into the world and find something to give us light so we may see one another, the land where we live, and the animals that feed us."

The sparrow flew away into the darkness. The little bird was gone so long that the raven thought it would never come back. Because there was no light, there was no day and night. There was no time, so the raven had no idea how long the sparrow had been gone. But one day he heard the beat of its wings and felt it perch on his hand. In its bill were two pieces of mica wrapped in leaves. One piece was light, and the other was dark.

The raven broke off a small piece of the light mica and threw it into the air. At once a strong light flooded the world and dazzled all its inhabitants. For the first time the people could look out over the land on which they lived. They saw the forests, the animals on the ground and in the sea, and the birds in the air. They delighted in all the beauty around them.

But the light was too strong. It dazzled them. So the raven broke off a piece of the dark mica and threw it into the air. At once the light grew dim. People could see without their eyes hurting, and eventually night came and gave them the rest they needed.

The people now needed shelter from wind and storms. So the raven taught them to build houses. The raven showed them how to

The kayak is an ancient mode of conveyance for the Inuit. With so many bodies of water bordering their homeland, a sturdy and reliable boat was essential.

make kayaks and umiaks so they might sail and hunt on the water.

But the people grew into many, as did the animals, and they were crowded on their small island. Only the sea was big.

One day an enormous black monster, unlike no other animal, rose from the sea. The people rowed to it in their kayaks and umiaks and tried to harpoon it. But none of the harpoons could pierce the monster's thick skin.

The raven watched the people's hopeless fight and said to the little sparrow, "Come with me and hover over the monster; I am going to hunt it in a kayak."

The raven paddled out. And while the sparrow hovered in the air, the raven harpooned and killed the monster.

The people rejoiced and towed the monster back to their village. They cut the body into small pieces and threw the pieces in all directions. Out in the sea, many islands grew from these pieces until they formed a great and enormous coast. Now there was room for the people and the animals. The raven called all the people together and spoke to them:

"I am your father. To me you owe your lives and your land. You must never forget me."

Then he flew into the sky. There he flung the rest of the mica, and light shot across the world like a great fire. Thus were sky and earth created.

This was the creation of the world and its people and the animals. But before all this came the raven, and before him the little sparrow.

FOR THOUSANDS OF YEARS, THE INUIT HAVE INHABITED BROAD EXPANSES OF the Arctic and Subarctic from eastern Siberia across North America to Greenland. Cleverly adapting to the environment, largely through hunting and fishing, they have thrived in a world of ice and bleak tundra—a land where the temperature can plunge to minus eighty degrees Fahrenheit. One community in Etah, Greenland, is located just 900 miles from the North Pole and is the northernmost human settlement on earth.

The homeland of the Inuit spans four nations—Greenland, Canada, Russia, and the coastal areas of Alaska. The Inuit were long known to the outside world as Eskimos, an Algonquian word once thought to mean "eaters of raw flesh." It is now believed that the obscure name may actually refer to snowshoes. In any case, the people refer to themselves as *Inuit*, which means "the people."

It is generally believed that the Inuit moved on foot and by dogsled across the Bering Strait from Siberia to North America between 3000 and 1000 B.C., long after the ancestors of other native North American peoples had migrated to the continent. Other scholars believe the time of migration may have been much earlier—between 6000 and 5000 B.C. The oldest known villages, dating from about 2000 B.C., have been found on the Aleutian Islands and in southwestern Alaska. The Inuit gradually spread eastward into northern Canada and Greenland.

Living over such a vast region, the Inuit came to be divided into three large groups: the Alaska Inuit, which includes the Yuik of Siberia; the Central Inuit, which includes those in northern Canada, Labrador, and Baffin Island; and the Greenland Inuit. The Central Inuit in Canada include peoples, such as the Labrador Inuit, who make their home on the coast across from Newfoundland to Hudson Bay and on southern Baffin Island. The Central Inuit also live on the far northern areas of Greenland, on Baffin Island, and around

The Inuit occupy more territory, including large expanses of Alaska and Canada, than any other native people in the world.

Hudson Bay. The Banks Island Inuit, a Central Inuit group, inhabit Banks Island, Victoria Island, and the other islands along Canada's central Arctic coast. The Mackenzie River Inuit, also a Central Inuit group, have long made their home along the Arctic coast of western Canada.

The Inuit speak several closely related languages in the Eskimoan language family. Eskimoan itself is divided into two branches, Sirenikski-Yupik and Inuit-Inupiaq. Sirenikski and Yupik are spoken in Siberia. Yupik is also spoken in southwestern Alaska. People in northern Alaska speak Inupiaq. In Canada the language is called Inuit, and in Greenland, Greenlandic.

In most parts of Greenland, as in Canada, the native word for "people" is *inuit*, but Greenlanders today generally refer to themselves as *Kalaallitt*, a term of Danish origin meaning the native people of Greenland. These various names continue to be used. But in 1977 the international native organization known as the Inuit Circumpolar Conference adopted local usages, and the Inuit has gained wide acceptance.

Although there are regional variations in the Inuit way of life, they have traditionally hunted, trapped, and fished. The Inuit culture of survival affected every aspect of life. People struggled to secure the food, clothing, and shelter necessary to survive under the very harsh conditions of the Arctic land, sea, and weather. The culture included language, arts, and games, along with singing and dancing, and storytelling. Parents and grandparents taught their children the skills and beliefs needed to endure and enjoy the cold reaches of the north.

For many generations, families have made their homes on stretches of flat, barren, and often windswept land in an unforgiving climate. Parents and unmarried children, as well as married sons and their wives and children, lived together to ensure a better chance of surviving. The oldest man able to hunt serves as the family head. During the winter, several families often come together in a settlement. However, during the summer, the families go their separate ways to hunt and fish. Homes varied by region. In Greenland and Alaska, the Inuit formed villages of stone or igloos. *Igloo* is an Inuit word meaning "house." In Siberia, they constructed houses with driftwood and soil. Depending on the season, igloos are made of walrus or sealskin, or blocks of snow. During the winter, the Inuit of central and eastern Canada have traditionally lived in dome-shaped igloos made of snow blocks.

The Inuit's skill in making homes, tools, weapons, and clothing from the often scarce materials available to them has enabled them to survive in the harsh land and climate of the north. Men hunt, fish, and build homes, while women make clothing and cook meals. The Inuit eat seals, walrus, whales, fish, and *muktuk*, the layer of fat under a whale's skin. They also hunt caribou and polar bears and smaller mammals, such as arctic foxes and snowshoe hares. The eggs and meat of ducks, geese, and seabirds are also eaten. Food is often frozen and eaten cooked or dried. Seals, especially important to many Inuit, provide food, skins for clothes, meat for sled dogs, and oil for fuel. The Inuit use practically every part of the animal—skins for clothes, homes, and boats and bones for weapons and tools. Before a hunt,

*N*ot the white of snow, but the tufted spikes of cotton grass fill this northern field.

people hold ceremonies in hopes of finding game, and they honor the animals that they have killed in rituals.

People travel over water in kayaks and umiaks. Covered with the skins of caribou or seals, a kayak carries one person who sits in an opening of the long, closed boat in the center. Gliding through the water in a kayak, a hunter can silently approach prey. Made of a wooden frame covered with walrus skins, an umiak is a large, open boat. The Inuit use umiaks to carry people and supplies on hunting trips. People rely on dogsleds pulled by a team of as many as fourteen huskies to journey over the snow-covered land and frozen water. Today, many Inuit use motorized boats and snowmobiles as well.

The People and the Land

> The great sea
> Has sent me adrift,
> It moves me as the weed in a great river,
> Earth and the great weather
> Move me,
> Have carried me away
> And move my inward parts with joy.

For many people, the Arctic is a cold and forbidding place, sprawling about 3,200 miles from Greenland across the expanse of northern Canada and the northern coast of Alaska to the eastern Aleutian Islands. Yet the Inuit have sustained themselves for generations in this seemingly bleak landscape that stretches from Siberia to

The tundra calls forth images of bleak landscapes and a monotonous expanse of snow. But the summer often remedies that, bringing a collage of colors.

Greenland, and from southeastern Labrador to the Queen Elizabeth Islands. The vast territory also embraces more than 2,000 miles of northern Alaskan coast and the Aleutian Island chain that extends more than 1,000 miles from southern Alaska. About 117,000 native people—51,000 in Greenland and Denmark, 43,000 in Alaska, 21,000 in Canada, and about 1,600 in Siberia—are scattered across the immense region.

Temperatures are eased somewhat along the coast of the Pacific Ocean and nearby waters, although unrelenting winds blast the coast. In most of the Arctic, however, winters are long, dark, and bitterly cold and the tundra is blanketed with a hard crust of ice and snow. Although some Inuit, especially in western Alaska, live in forested areas, most communities are well north of the timberline. Hugging the ground, dwarf flowers, mosses, and lichens flourish during the brief warmth and light of summer. During the summer, the flat land is usually spongy, due to poor drainage and the permafrost, a layer of ice beneath the surface that never thaws. Mosquitoes, black flies, and other biting insects breed in the shallow pools of water that collect on the tundra. Rising up in great, blood-sucking swarms, the mosqitoes attack people and caribou.

Despite all the ice and snow that collects on the surface, most of the Arctic is actually an arid region with as little as four inches of precipitation a year. The exceptions are in Labrador and southwestern Alaska which receive a good bit of rain carried by the ocean winds. For water, the Inuit rely on ocean ice, which loses much of its salt content in a year or so of being frozen. Otherwise, the Inuit and other native peoples of the far north would never have enough freshwater.

Living primarily along the coastline and offshore islands, the Inuit became skilled hunters on land and sea. They came to understand the subtle changes in the land, sea, and ice that made up their world. Their quarry included sea mammals, notably seals, walruses, narwhal, and whales. While seals were essential to the survival of some Inuit groups, caribou were the most vital source of food for others, especially during spring and autumn migrations of the caribou. The Inuit hunted other land mammals for meat or fur. They also shot birds and gathered eggs from nests. In some regions of the north, they picked berries. They caught large numbers of fish with hooks, nets, spears, and traps. Though their homeland is in one of the world's harshest environments, they found many ways not only to survive, but to establish a flourishing culture.

2. Communities

Skins and wooden stakes provided
the Inuit with a simple home.
Often the shelter was banked
with stones to keep out the
North's harsh weather.

THE INUIT TRADITIONALLY LIVED IN SMALL, ISOLATED VILLAGES SCATTERED widely over the snowy expanses. Some villages may have had as many as eight hundred inhabitants, especially if game was abundant in the region. However, most communities consisted of groups of ten to fifty people who were usually related by blood or marriage. Each of these camps had one to six dwellings in which men, women, and children lived together.

Because they had to devote so much time and energy to hunting and protecting themselves from the bitter cold, the Inuit did not form complex social and political organizations. The basic social unit was the family, which usually consisted of the husband and the wife and their two or three children. At one time, it was thought that the small number of children in Inuit families was due to infanticide, the practice of intentionally allowing a baby to die, or a high infant mortality rate because of the harsh climate. However, it is more likely that Inuit women simply had fewer children for a number of reasons. Women breast-fed their children until they were five or six years old—or sometimes even older. While breast-feeding, they were less likely to get pregnant again. Because of food shortages and the rigors of life, women also had greater difficulty in getting pregnant. Or they frequently had miscarriages, especially when they undertook arduous travel and tasks, such as hauling and butchering caribou and other large animals. In the early twentieth century, as the Inuit became more settled and women began to wean their children at a younger age, the birth rate increased.

Inuit families must rely on each other, if they are to survive the rigors of the Arctic.

Occasionally, some Inuit did allow a newborn to die, especially if harsh conditions made it impossible to care for the baby. They let the baby freeze to death, but only before they had given it a name, since they believed that a body without a name was not yet a human being. However, such measures were undertaken only in the most desperate situations, for example, when the family was facing starvation. At all other times, children were cherished as a way to continue the life of the family, provide care for parents in old age, and to bring joy to their families. Both the very old and the very young enhanced the community. The Inuit loved to be surrounded by other people, especially other family members. Living together for years, often in close quarters, people knew each other so well that a slight gesture or change in expression could communicate a thought or feeling.

Family life could become very complicated, especially when the fifty or so people in a settlement were all members of a single family. Traditionally, people relied on their extended families. Many men had two or three wives and, in some regions, women occasionally had two husbands. Because of the multiple marriages, relationships became even more complicated. Inuit families had fewer children and more adult relatives than typical Western families. Relatives and in-laws often acted as though they were members of a nuclear family of parents and children. Cousins often viewed each other as brother and sister. Aunts and uncles often treated nieces and nephews as their own children.

Elders were honored for their wisdom and knowledge of customs and taboos, as well as for their skill as storytellers. Many Westerners once thought that the Inuit viewed the elderly as a burden. It is true that during a famine an aged person might wander out into a snowstorm to freeze to death, so that the small amount of food on hand would be left for the young and strong. When people moved to another hunting ground, an old person who could no longer carry heavy loads might also decide to be left behind. But the Inuit valued the lives of everyone in the community. They believed that death was a passing of the soul from one body to another. When an old woman sacrificed herself to the freezing cold, people believed that her soul would soon come back in a newborn baby. The family gave her name to the next baby born and, in the ensuing weeks, people might note how the infant displayed traits and manners similar to those of the old woman. To the Inuit, all lives were bound in an ever-renewing cycle.

Family members formed especially strong cooperative bonds as they worked together to provide food, clothing, and shelter. Hunters were honored to share their meat with others in the group. If one group went on a hunting expedition and abandoned a house, others were allowed to seek shelter there. However, the Inuit sense of cooperation posed difficulties in relating with Europeans. The Inuit generally trusted other people and thus were often cheated by dishonest traders. When it came to dealing with the nations that claimed sovereignty over them, the Inuit, without a strong political organization, often could not understand the language and treaty terms, let alone negotiate with the representatives of these governments.

The Inuit did rely on strong leaders and a hierarchical structure within the family in managing their daily lives. Parents had authority over their children. Elders also generally had more influence over younger members of the group, although they served primarily as advisers. The men made most of the decisions, especially when moving the camp. However, this authority was often expressed

Relatives often gather in groups to better provide themselves with food, clothing, and shelter.

through respect rather than orders. For instance, a father might say, "We are getting low on seal meat," instead of directly telling his son to go hunting. If a father said, "I'm thirsty," that meant the younger son was expected to fetch him a drink of water.

People traced their descent through both sides of their family. Kinship was critically important. Strangers who could not establish their relationship with the group were considered hostile and might even be killed. Yet cooperation was also necessary and unrelated people often came together to hunt, trade, and even avenge a death. They also enjoyed visiting other families. They often came together to play games and share stories, as well as to hold festivals and feasts, all of which strengthened the bonds of unity. Sometimes, men exchanged their wives for brief periods of time. Families shared the labor of moving to new hunting grounds.

Dwellings

Depending on where they lived, the Inuit made two kinds of winter homes. Central Inuit usually built snow igloos. They often attached several igloos for greater warmth and to provide separate quarters for living, sleeping, and storage. Men first cut blocks of wind-hardened snow and laid the blocks as a foundation, a circle about ten to fifteen feet in diameter. They then stacked rows of blocks, each succeeding row placed slightly inward to make a dome shape. They briefly melted the surface of the inside wall with the heat of a blubber lamp known as a *kudlik*. The surface quickly froze again into a windproof glaze. The Inuit often added a small porch for storage and a window

*T*he Inuit built homes called igloos with the material that was most readily available—blocks of wind-hardened snow.

of clear ice. For ventilation, they left a small hole at the top of the dome. To enter or exit the snow house, people crawled through a long, low tunnel that kept cold air from blowing into the house. Inside, they made benches and tables of hard-packed snow. Platforms covered with warm furs and willow branches, if available, served as beds. For light and heat, women tended a small blubber lamp over which they placed a cooking pot or drying rack.

Igloos were common, especially among the Inuit who lived in northern Canada where snow is plentiful. However, many people used igloos only as temporary shelters. Most Inuit, especially those living in Greenland and Alaska, constructed a square or oblong house known as a *karmat*. These earth dwellings consisted of a wood or whale bone frame built over a shallow pit. The frame was covered with sod. As with an igloo, people entered through a tunnel, although in some regions, they used a passageway through the roof. Occasionally they stretched clear animal gut over small openings to make windows. Another important building was a large ceremonial house for the men, which was known in western Alaska as the *kashim*. During the summer, the Inuit lived in tents made by covering driftwood or whale bone frames with seal or caribou skins.

The Inuit often lived in summer homes made of driftwood or whale bone frames covered with seal or caribou skins.

3. Lifeways

Games are an essential part of Inuit life. Here a child goes flying through the air.

IN THE ARCTIC, PEOPLE FORMED CLOSE FAMILIES AND TIGHTLY KNIT SOCIAL groups to better their chances of survival. If a man had no wife to sew and cook for him, he became a burden to his family. Without good clothes, he froze when he hunted in the winter. Without a husband, a woman had no one to provide meat for meals and hides for clothes. When a man and woman married, they were able to help each other. Their children also helped to provide for the family. The success of future generations depended on raising healthy and strong individuals who were able to provide for themselves and each other.

Cycle of Life

Birth. During a pregnancy, a woman often worried about the uncertain future. Would the baby come during a blizzard or a time of starvation when people were migrating over the tundra? Would she have a boy who would take care of her in old age or a girl for whom she would have to find a good match someday? Would she and the baby live or perish during childbirth?

If the woman went into labor on the trail, she would drop behind and have her baby, often alone. She tried to have the baby as quickly as possible and then catch up with the others. While she recovered, the new mother was allowed to ride in a sled with her baby tucked warmly inside the *amaut*, or hood, of her coat. Yet, in most instances, the woman did not give birth alone. Her husband and one or two women, serving as midwives, helped with the delivery. If there were complications, a shaman, or *angakok*, was brought in to ask the spirits, or *inuas*, for help.

The woman gave birth in a kneeling position. If the group was not on the move, she rested indoors for several days to regain her strength. During this time, her other children were sent to stay with friends or family. The Inuit observed various taboos after a child was born. The mother had to make a fire under a cooking pot as soon as possible—to ensure that her child would learn to walk at an early age. A friend or relative also stretched the legs to help the child grow tall. Whenever the mother ate she had to rub a little food on her baby's cheek to ensure that he or she would never go hungry.

A *family was overjoyed at the birth of a new baby.*

The mother of a newborn could not eat from the common pot. She had to have her own cooking pot and bowl. Her cooking pot could not be traded or given away until her child was fully grown. Similarly, the baby's first ritual clothing, often a caribou skin robe, was carefully stored away. The umbilical cord was kept as an amulet. If any of these objects were to be lost, it was believed that the child would die.

The Inuit always remembered the day on which a child was born. They recalled everyone who was present at the birth. They knew if a snowstorm had been raging or if the dogs had been howling in the wind that day. All of these details formed the first chapter of a person's life story.

Babies usually wore no clothes except for an animal skin diaper. For the first few months, they were kept warm and safe inside the *amaut* of their mother's coat. Children did not receive their first clothes—a one-piece suit with a flap in the back for diaper changing—until they were old enough to walk. Mittens, which were attached to the suit, and sealskin shoes completed the outfit.

Parents cherished their babies. A mother snuggled her infant within her heavy coat. She carried her baby wherever she went. The baby slept with her and breast-fed whenever it was hungry for at least three years but usually longer. As the Inuit's diet is composed mostly of meat, weaning was gradual. The mother first gave broth and boiled fish to her baby. Later, she fed the infant seal or caribou meat that she had chewed.

Childhood. Most Inuit named their children immediately after birth, although some people waited a few days. Friends and family suggested names to the parents who generally named their child after a relative who had recently passed away. Most people had two names. Sometimes, a person was called one name by the family and another by outsiders. Occasionally people acquired nicknames as well.

Although they were often busy, parents attentively cared for their children and seldom punished them. Children had the run of the camp, where they were generally safe as everyone knew them and helped watch over them. Parents instructed their children to be patient and cheerful. Obedience and hard work were encouraged by everyone in the community.

Even as they have embraced news ways, the Inuit have continued to raise their children in the traditions of their ancestors.

Children learned many important skills needed for survival. Mothers taught their daughters how to cook meals and sew clothing. Fathers taught their sons—and occasionally their daughters—how to hunt and fish. Parents lavished praise on their children when they excelled at any of these tasks.

Children also played with toys, such as little sleds to which they harnessed puppies. With their own small-scale bows and arrows, they practiced archery by shooting at blocks of snow. They pretended to drive caribou into pits and used sticks for kayaks. Girls enjoyed playing with dolls. They also sewed with needles and tended toy lamps made from small pieces of soapstone. In Alaska, a father often carved a "story knife" for his daughter from a walrus tusk or driftwood. As she drew pictures of animals, people, and everyday activities in the snow, the girl made up stories that she shared with her friends.

Coming-of-Age. The warm clothing—parka, trousers, boots— was important not only for cold weather but spiritual protection as children grew up. The Inuit often sewed amulets to their clothes to ward off evil spirits and provide guidance. For instance, it was believed that a flipper bone from a ringed seal would help a young man become a good hunter. A piece of fish skin assisted a young woman in becoming skilled at sewing. Other amulets included the hair of an old man to ensure long life, a raven skin to make one invisible when hunting, and the head of a red-throated loon to help

*T*raditionally, when an Inuit woman came of age she was ready to marry. It was essential that her husband be a good provider.

in fishing. Boys also often grew their hair long as protection against spiritual dangers.

Girls generally wore the same kind of clothes until they were married. Boys usually began to wear men's clothing when they came of age and began to hunt and fish with their fathers.

Marriage. Girls usually married before their first menstrual period. In marriage, romance mattered less than the skills of a woman and the hunting ability of the man. Sometimes, marriages were arranged in advance by the parents, but young people were not bound to these betrothals. When they came of age, they could marry whomever they wished. There was no special wedding ceremony. The couple simply decided to live together, and they were considered to be married. They either set up their own household or, if young, went to live with the man's parents for a while, often in an addition to the house. The man worked hard to show that he was a good provider. A man was proud if he could feed his wife well enough that she became plump, considered a sign of beauty. Divorce was as simple as marriage—the couple separated without any ceremony. Marriages could be fragile at the beginning, but most couples stayed together, especially after the birth of the first child.

Death. Inuit life was hard, and few people lived to old age. Men usually died in their mid-forties and women in their mid-fifties. For the few people who lived long enough, old age was considered a misery. Sometimes crippled, toothless, and nearly blind, old people became a burden to themselves and their families. When food was scarce and people had to move camp, an elderly mother or father might stay behind in a little snow house that served as both shelter and tomb. Similarly, during hard times, baby girls were occasionally left to die in the snow because the family could not afford to keep them. Boys were spared because they would ultimately grow old enough to become hunters who could provide game and fish. Among some groups, such as the Caribou Inuit of central Canada, women outnumbered men because of the high male mortality through hunting accidents.

The Inuit respected and feared the dead. They believed that the spirit of the deceased would become evil and seek revenge on the living. It was thought that dead people who had not been treated properly hated the living and brought winter storms and starvation. Among one Inuit group, the Copper Inuit, the body of the deceased was bound with thongs to keep its spirit from harming others. Following the death of a man the body lay in a house or tent for three days. If a woman died her body lay for four days. During this time people mourned and observed many taboos. They could not sew or comb their hair. At night they laid knives between the body and the rest of the household, perhaps to protect themselves as they slept from the dead person's spirit.

After the period of mourning, a hole was cut in the back wall of the house or tent and the body was removed. It was believed that no other spirits should observe the family taking away the deceased. The house and belongings of the deceased were then abandoned. Unable

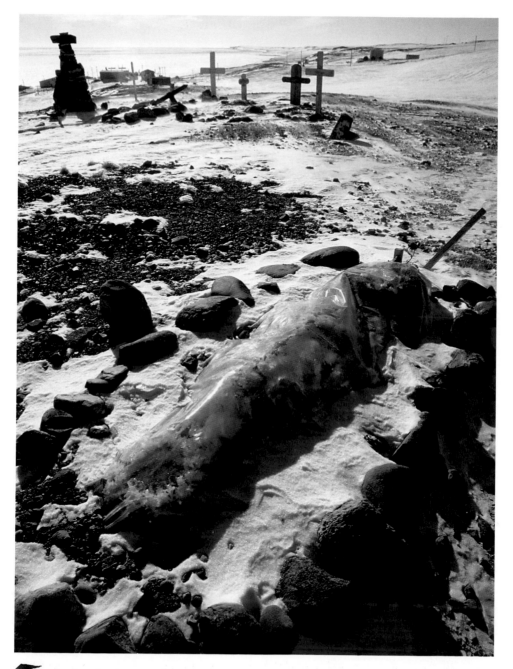

*T*he body of a loved one is encircled with stones. Sheets of plastic are often used to protect flowers and other offerings for the deceased.

to dig a grave in the rocky, frozen ground, people laid the body in a circle of small stones and covered with stones and driftwood. The Copper Inuit, however, left the body uncovered. They cut the thongs that bound the body to release the spirit of the dead person. Finally, they placed some or all of the deceased's belongingss with the body for use in the afterlife.

After the funeral, anyone who had handled the body had to drink water when they arrived home, so the deceased would not be thirsty. They also had to give a piece of blubber from the first animal killed after the burial to every person in the village. Each person then burned the blubber in a lamp.

Some Inuit had taboos against speaking the dead person's name. They occasionally visited the grave. However, if the person had died violently, they believed the grave might be haunted by an evil spirit and they stayed away.

Hunting and Fishing

With few edible plants in the Arctic, the Inuit sustained themselves mostly by hunting and fishing. Men spent most of each day in pursuit of whales, seals, or caribou. They also hunted walruses, sea lions, and narwhals that had migrated north in the warmer months. Whether hunting seals or whales, men used basically the same equipment—harpoons to which lines and air-filled sealskin floats were attached. Sometimes, a man working alone could spear a small whale or seal from his kayak. Along the Pacific coast of Alaska, men speared whales with poison-tipped lances, then went home and undertook rituals intended to kill the whale magically. Other men watched the whale as it swam through the water. As the poison worked through its body, the whale eventually died, but often far away from where it had been speared. Whales speared by hunters in one village often floated to the surface or washed ashore near another village. However, as whales were plentiful, there was enough food for everyone living along the coast.

In the eastern Arctic, groups of men in kayaks hunted large bowhead whales. Each man tried to thrust a harpoon into the whale's head. Exhausted by dragging many floats, the whale had to surface where the men then attempted to kill it with spears. However, men were often able to thrust only one or two harpoons and many whales escaped. In Greenland and northwestern Alaska, men hunted more effectively in crews paddling umiaks. Each crew usually had six paddlers, a harpooner, and a helmsman who steered the boat. Unlike a single hunter who had to paddle and steer his kayak while trying to throw a harpoon, each man in the umiak could concentrate on his assigned task. Using both hands, the harpooner drove a sturdy harpoon into the whale in a powerful and precise thrust. Three or four floats were attached to the harpoon to ensure that the whale would soon tire. When exhausted from dragging the floats, the whale surfaced. Men then speared the whale and towed its body to shore.

In parts of Alaska and southwestern Greenland, the ocean never freezes. However, everywhere else in the polar north, the sea freezes for at least half of the year. During the winter, when boats could not be used, men usually hunted seals from ice floes, waiting at breathing

Living at the edge of the ocean, the Inuit harpooned seals and pursued giant whales.

holes called *aglus*. Sea mammals have to periodically come up for air and hunters often relied on a dog to sniff out the breathing holes that were usually covered with snow and nearly invisible. Since larger sea mammals migrated southward, the Inuit mainly hunted seals during the winter. Floats dragged by harpooned animals, called drag floats, could not be used on the ice, so men had to harpoon the seal directly in the head. Men hunted as a group, each patiently guarding one of the many holes in the ice. A man might watch his breathing hole for hours in the dark and intense cold for a single, fleeting chance to catch a single seal. In warmer seasons, the men stalked seals on the ice or harpooned them from kayaks.

A man waited hours, often days, for a seal to bob up in a breathing hole. If he missed, he would have to begin the vigil all over again. Some people, such as the Copper Inuit of the central Arctic, hunted in groups. Moving the entire village onto the ice a few miles from shore, they placed a hunter at each breathing hole. If every breathing hole was covered, a seal was likely to be caught by at least one hunter. When most of the seals had been hunted at one location, the village moved to another site.

When the sun began to appear again in the spring, seals began to crawl out onto the ice and warm themselves next to their breathing holes. Raising their heads every minute or so, the seals kept careful watch. A hunter had to crawl over the ice on his belly, pretending to be another seal. When the seal raised its head, the hunter either lay perfectly still like a seal sunning itself or raised his head like a seal looking around. He might stalk a seal for several hours only to see the

An Inuit man inspects a breathing hole in the ice. A hunter often waited patiently for hours for a seal to surface.

Among the fiercest and most dangerous animals stalked by the Inuit were walruses, such as this huge bull claimed by hunters.

seal slip into the water when he was just a few yards away. Or he might be lucky enough to spear the seal with his harpoon.

Hunting was often dangerous. Bowhead whales could easily capsize an umiak with a single sweep of their tails. Humpback and gray whales of the Pacific even attacked small boats. With their sharp tusks, walruses were especially dangerous. Although smaller than most whales, a bull walrus can still weigh more than an entire umiak crew—and a bull walrus is quite fierce. It will viciously charge not only a man hunting alone but also large boats. Walruses also gather in pods of dozens or even hundreds of animals, so hunting had to be undertaken with the utmost care. Even then, hunters were often killed by these aggressive mammals.

In many areas, such as the interior of northwestern Alaska, the barrens west of Hudson Bay, and stretches of land in northern Canada, the caribou was the Inuit's main source of food. Also known as the North American reindeer, caribou provided not only meat but hides for shelter, clothing, and boats, as well as sinew for thread. Large numbers of these animals migrated across the northern part of the mainland, while smaller herds lived in the ice-free areas of Greenland and on many of the islands of northern Canada.

Always on the move, caribou wintered south of the timberline and migrated to the tundra during warmer weather. When the herds returned north in the summer, men ambushed them—either by creeping up or hiding in a pit until the caribou passed by. They could never be sure of the route to be taken by the caribou, but they observed weather conditions and consulted with shamans. They also knew that caribou frequented certain routes, such as shallow river crossings and valleys through hills and mountains. Cooperating in group hunts, men stacked piles of rocks, or cairns, in a large V shape that narrowed at the edge of the water or a corral. As the caribou approached the wide part of the V, women and children, who had been in hiding, shouted and waved their arms, driving the herd into the V. If the cairns ended at a river, men waiting in kayaks speared or shot the caribou with bows and arrows as they plunged into the current. After they had killed enough animals, they retrieved the carcasses floating in the water. If the cairns were located on land, the Inuit built a corral at the narrow end and caught the caribou there with snares made of the skins of walrus or seals.

Fish were also a vital source of food, especially to the Inuit of Alaska. Men caught fish with hooks and lines, nets, and spears. Many Alaskan Inuit fished all winter with gill nets placed under the ice. Fish, such as the Arctic cod in areas of Alaska and the capelin of the Atlantic, from time to time washed ashore in large numbers. People simply had to scoop them up in baskets. Favorite kinds of freshwater fish included trout, grayling, blackfish, and pike. People caught halibut, tomcod, capelin, herring, and sharks in the ocean. In southwestern Alaska, people also caught eels. The most important fish were those that migrated from the sea to freshwater, such as Arctic char and several kinds of whitefish and salmon. To catch migratory fish, the Inuit often built weirs. These weirs consisted of two stone dams or fences across the river where the fish were ascending. An opening was left in the lower, or downstream, dam. When enough fish had swum through the opening and were blocked by the second weir, men closed the opening. People then waded into the water and speared the fish. Instead of weirs, people in the western Arctic— usually women—used nets made of lines of sealskin, willow bark, or shredded baleen to catch migrating fish.

People not only ate caribou, seals, walruses, and whales, but also many kinds of fish, including halibut and salmon.

In preparing animals and fish for meals, women needed sturdy tools, such as this blade used for cleaning and scraping meat.

Pacific salmon die after spawning, but char and Atlantic salmon, after wintering in lakes and rivers, head to the sea again in early summer. Some Inuit caught fish during these migrations. In the western Arctic, whitefish and freshwater grayling move downriver in the autumn. To catch these fish, some Inuit built a fence with a narrow gate across a stream. They placed a basket with a cone-shaped opening over the gate. Fish swam into the basket but then could not easily swim out again. The construction of the fence required considerable labor, but afterward the fisherman only had to periodically raise and empty the basket filled with fish.

Depending on where they lived, Inuit bands hunted many other kinds of animals besides seals and caribou. These included musk oxen, mountain sheep, grizzly bears, polar bears, lynx, wolves, wolverines, and fox. Depending on the place and the season, they also caught sea otters, river otters, muskrats, marmots, hares, and ground squirrels. Over many generations, men perfected their methods and weapons for catching these animals. They hunted them from blinds and trapped them in snares, deadfalls, and weighted nets. They also used three or four kinds of arrows, as well as a dozen varied kinds of spears or harpoons, each of which was ideally suited for hunting a particular mammal, bird, or fish.

To supplement their diet, some Inuit also harvested crabs, shellfish, and sea urchins. During the spring and summer, they gathered the eggs of ducks, geese, swans, and seabirds nesting in the cliffs. Snowy owls were occasionally cooked in soups and in some locales ptarmigan were a source of food during the late winter. Yet the Inuit's survival largely depended on their ability to gather and store large amounts of meat and fish during brief summer seasons. Whether whale, seal, or caribou, the meat was fairly divided among the people according to time-honored rules. The Inuit cut the flesh into strips and allowed them to dry for two or three days. In the far north they stored frozen carcasses under piles of rocks. The Inuit of

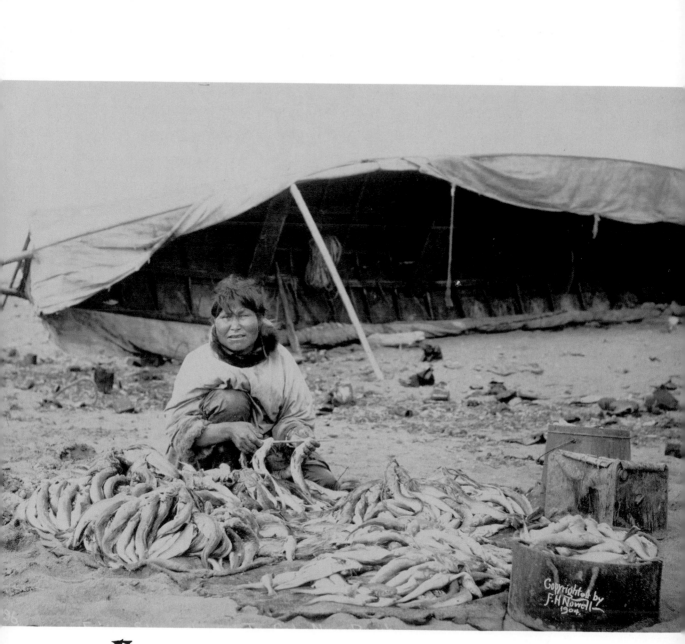

F*ish were eaten raw or often dried for later use. Here, a woman strings a large pile of cod to be dried at her campsite.*

Alaska dug pits that served as cellars in the frozen ground. People often ate fish and meat raw and cooked only the toughest pieces. The Inuit never wasted any part of their fish and game. They ate the flesh and used the skins and bones to make tools, weapons, and shelters. Blubber was an especially important resource for light, heat, and medicine, as well as for food. Stored out of direct sunlight, cubes of seal blubber melted into a clear liquid similar to vegetable oil. Melted blubber was eaten and burned in lamps for heat and light. When game was scarce, the Inuit might have to eat their clothing, even their dogs. The word *ajurnamat*, which means "it cannot be helped," reflects the Inuit's patience and acceptance of fate. However, during good times they enjoyed great feasts.

Making Meals

The Inuit believed that food tasted better when shared with family and friends. Sharing reminded people of the critical need for cooperation. When people ate together, they felt a deeper sense of appreciation for everyone around them. Strangers became friends when offered a meal. Celebrations centered around a great feast with lots of fresh meat or frozen fish that had been cached for the long, sunless days of winter. At these gatherings, people chatted, laughed, and told stories. To this day, people enjoy coming together for community feasts that include plenty of traditional foods. Everyone gathers in a public place to enjoy food donated by different families. In larger communities, much of the food is provided by specially chosen hunters.

In one feast, known as *alupajaq*, the Inuit continue to honor the traditions of their ancestors. The men gather around a seal that is to be eaten. Two or three men ritually cut up the animal, while the women remain in a group several feet away. They listen as the men tell hunting stories. The women talk happily about the seal and the good fortune of being blessed with plenty. The meat is passed from the men to the women, with the choicest parts given to the women. First come the upper flippers, which two women cut into pieces for everyone. Slivers of the heart are then passed around the group. These are followed by the liver. The tender meat on the upper spine is shared by the women while the men take the meat from the lower spine. The women next accept the front ribs and the men take the back ribs. Guests take care to leave part of the seal for their generous hosts, although they are often encouraged to take some of the meat home. Expressing their thanks, some guests politely leave as soon as they have eaten, even before washing up. They do not wish to take up too much room and overstay their welcome. The remaining guests help in cleaning up after the meal.

Traditionally, the Inuit ate meat frozen or with a variety of sauces, such as *aalu*, *misiraq*, and *nirukkaq* as flavorings. Aalu was—and still is—made from lean, choice cuts of caribou or seal meat that have been cut into small pieces and mixed with a little melted fat, animal blood, and ptarmigan intestine. Women mix the ingredients briskly with their fingers until it becomes frothy. Aalu is one of the most popular dips for many kinds of meat. Misiraq is made from seal or whale blubber. Stored in a cool place, the blubber is allowed to age until it becomes a clear, aromatic liquid. Nirukkaq is made with the contents of a caribou stomach that have been frozen, thawed, and cleaned of bits of grass and lichens. People use nirukkaq as a dip for caribou meat.

Traditionally, the Inuit also ate dried fish and meats, such as caribou. By strict custom, caribou stew had to be prepared on land. The dish was often cooked with blackberry canes to give the meat a pleasant woody smell and taste. Over the past century, the Inuit have adapted new recipes for caribou and fish that include spices. The Inuit also occasionally ate greens such as chard, if they were available. They gathered wild potatoes, flowers, and berries, and dug the roots of some plants. However, their diet consisted mainly of meat and fats that provided the strength and energy needed to hunt and fish in the intense cold.

The Inuit enjoyed many other dishes. In a cookbook compiled by the students of the Shishmaref Day School in western Alaska in 1952, recipes for many kinds of fish and animals, including loons and owls, are included, along with a treat known as Eskimo Ice Cream. This dish was made by grating reindeer tallow into tiny pieces. While beating by hand, the cook added seal oil and then a little water, continuing to do so until the mixture became white and fluffy. Berries were then added to make a tasty dessert.

Here is a modern recipe that includes fish and other ingredients traditionally eaten by the Inuit.

Seafood Chowder

Ingredients

1 and 1/2 cups clams

2 and 1/2 lbs. assorted fish (halibut, salmon, cod, or other fish)

1/2 cup shelled crab meat

5 strips bacon

2 onions, finely chopped

2 stalks of finely chopped celery

6 to 8 medium-sized potatoes, peeled and cubed

2 cans chicken broth

1/2 teaspoon salt

1/4 teaspoon pepper

1 can evaporated milk

1 cup milk

8 tablespoons of flour

Dice the bacon and fry in a large pot until crisp and brown. Add chicken broth, onion, celery, clams, crab, potatoes, and seasonings. Bring mixture to a boil and cook until potatoes are tender. Add cubed fish and simmer for five minutes. Be careful not to overcook the fish.

Blend flour, evaporated milk, and regular milk. Pour this mixture into pot and heat until the chowder thickens. Do not allow the liquid to come to a boil. Add additional pepper to taste and serve.

Clothing and Jewelry

The Alaska Inuit who lived in the mild climate along the Pacific coast had to contend with rain and wind but not much cold. They dressed lightly in a long pullover shirt with a high collar and a tightly fitting neck. Over the shirt, they often wore a hooded, waterproof windbreaker known as a *kamleika*. However, most Inuit had to wear clothing suitable for the intense cold of the north, or they would quickly freeze to death.

Inuit clothes had to be warm and waterproof. Without them, people would never have survived the bitterly cold winters.

Basic attire included a hooded parka, heavy trousers, boots, and mittens. Although men and women wore the same outfits, the styles varied between the sexes. In some regions, women's pants and boots were sewn together to make one garment. Women made summer clothes of waterproof sealskin and winter clothes of warm, yet light-weight caribou hide. They also used the fur of other animals, including polar bears, wolves, foxes, dogs, marmots, and squirrels, as well as bird feathers, in making clothing. In the winter, people generally wore two garments—an inner suit with the fur turned toward the skin and an outer parka with the fur out. Parkas fit snugly around the wrists, waist, and neck to keep out the cold. Women's parkas occasionally included a warm, fur-lined *amaut* to carry babies. Called *mukluks* or *kamiks*, boots had moss or down between each of four layers of caribou hide or sealskin for warmth. Women's boots went all the way up the thigh, while men's boots were shorter.

Early explorers thought the Inuit were fat, but their bulky clothing only made them appear to be heavy. The layers of winter clothing were so remarkably warm that the Inuit could sleep out-doors, in an outfit weighing only about ten pounds, even when the temperature plunged to sixty degrees below zero. The clothing was so well insulated that it became a shelter when men went on hunting trips for two or three days. At night, they simply built a windbreak of snow and hunkered down inside their warm parkas.

From an early age, women learned to sew the seams of clothing tightly with sinew so that garments would repel water. In the Arctic,

Women occasionally adorned themselves with jewelry, including earrings and nose rings, made from ivory and shells.

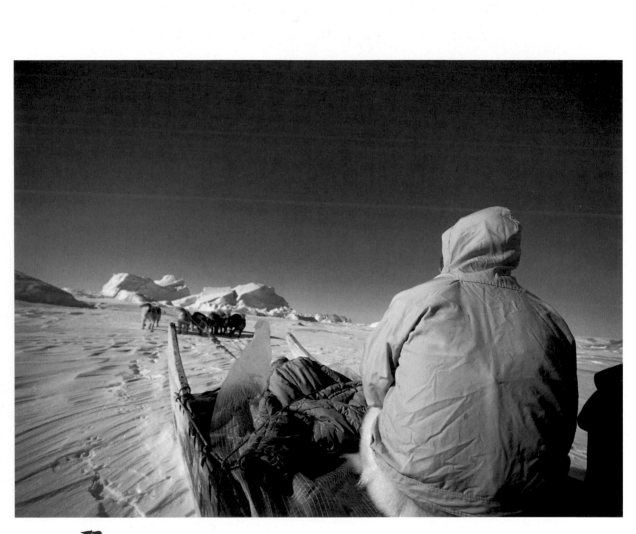

*P*eople could travel and transport goods swiftly over the windswept snow on dog sleds pulled by teams of sturdy huskies.

staying dry was essential. A person who got wet quickly froze to death. However, the clothing was so well sewn that it could not breathe. Moisture, including perspiration, condensed on the skin. So, the Inuit had to continually dry their clothing. As soon as they came from a hunt, men brushed the snow off their clothes before entering the warm home. Once inside, they quickly shed the outside layer of their clothing which the women turned inside out and carefully dried over a blubber lamp. Women then chewed the boots and beat other clothes with a stick if they had gotten stiff.

People dressed for special occasions in clothing trimmed with fur and embroidered with designs. Among the Copper Inuit, men's dance regalia was often adorned with lemming skins. Women often had an extensive wardrobe that included both everyday clothes and fancier dance outfits. Many people wore *atagtat*, or amulets, as sacred objects on their clothing to bring good fortune. For instance, it was believed that wolf bones helped men to become strong and clever hunters. Some groups also wore jewelry—earrings, nose rings, and lip plugs—fashioned from ivory, shells, sandstone, or wood. Many men and women also sported tattoos as a form of decoration.

Handicrafts

The Inuit once made the tools, weapons, and other goods they needed to survive in the far north. With few trees in the Arctic, they had to use driftwood, stones, bones, and antlers. Sometimes, they traveled hundreds of miles to find suitable stones. They chipped the stones—flint, slate, and quartz—to make scrapers, points for arrows, harpoons, and spears, and knife blades, including the special curved blades for the knives known as *ulus*. Driftwood was made into tool and weapon handles as well as house and boat frames, boxes, and dishes. They fashioned various kinds of harpoons and spears known as *atlatls*. Men also skillfully wove nets and made snares for small animals. Caribou sinew was used as thread and fishing line. They shaped bones and antlers into weapons, notably harpoons and bows and arrows, and many tools, including knives, axes, scrapers, drills, thimbles, and needles. In their daily tasks, women relied most heavily on needles made of bone or ivory, sinew-backed knives, and chipped stone scrapers.

Men built light, yet sturdy kayaks and umiaks for paddling over the icy waters. To make these boats they laid out a wooden frame lashed together with sinew. They sheathed the frame with sewn caribou or sealskins. A hole was left in the top of the kayaks for the propeller. Kayaks were propelled with a paddle with a blade on each end. Men used kayaks mainly for hunting. Because of their slender, graceful design, kayaks could be paddled swiftly and silently and were easily maneuvered in the water. Umiaks were large, open boats used for transportation and whaling. Men also made sleds pulled by hardy northern dogs known as huskies for travel during the winter. They lashed the wood frame together with strips of rawhide and made runners of wood or bone. They coated the runners with moss and ice so the dogsled would glide smoothly over the snow.

Artistry

The Inuit were not only skilled craftspeople, they were also talented artists. They expressed themselves through a variety of arts, from sculpture to singing. The arts were viewed as a means of achieving inner joy. Many Inuit carved pieces of bone, antler, or ivory into imaginative figurines, amulets, toys, and other small objects. Some groups also carved and painted wooden masks for dances and other ceremonies. Women artfully sewed furs into clothing not only for warmth but as decorations on the garment. These objects were never intended to be exhibited—they were part of the everyday life and special ceremonies of the Inuit.

The Inuit were also known for their singing. People sang as they worked and as they played games. They sang as they danced or told stories. They sang to make fun of each other and to soothe frightened children. They sang about love and revenge, as well as hunting and animals. Songs were performed in a deep, nasal voice, which is sometimes called "throat singing." People gathered in their igloos and rejoiced through songs when they had enough food. They also sang during the lean days of the bleakest winter as in this song:

> Hard times, dearth times
> Plague us every one.
> Stomachs are shrunken,
> Dishes are empty
> Ayaa, yaa, yapape!
> Ayaa, yaa, yapape!

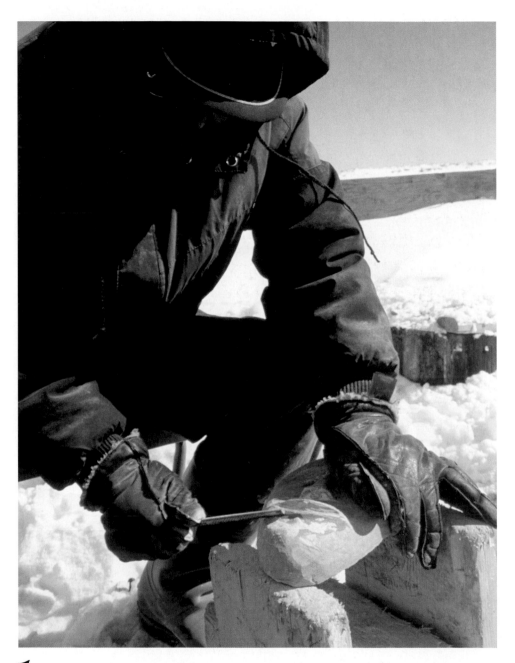

*I*nuit sculptors enjoyed carving small objects from bone, antler, and ivory, as well as ceremonial wooden masks.

Some songs were rooted in the Inuit's ancient origins, while others were composed spontaneously for feasts and festivals. Songs could belong to a person, family, or community. Whatever their nature, songs were heard everywhere, especially at dances. Among the Inuit who lived in the east, one man stood in the middle of the room and sang while in a state of ecstasy he danced and beat a drum. When he became exhausted, he passed the instrument to the next man and the dance continued.

Among the Inuit in the west, people often danced in groups. These dances varied in complexity among the people of Alaska and other regions. Dances included those with choreographed movements and those with no set movements. There were also sitting and kneeling dances in which people moved only their arms and heads.

They danced to entertain themselves and to illustrate stories. Dance was also a feature of special ceremonies such as the wolf dance. The wolf dance had several formal parts in which women and men faced each other. The women held wands adorned with feathers, and men wore headdresses of loon skin and long mittens.

Games

The Inuit enjoyed many games. In the hopping game girls and boys competed to see who could hop on one foot the longest. During the brief warmth of summer, three or four people used an animal skin as a trampoline. As they jumped up and down, children learned to do tricks in the air. Children also played raven, a game similar to tag. One child, flapping his or her arms and cawing like a raven,

*T*he traditional arts of the Inuit are still practiced to this day, as is evident in this female Yupik speaker doll.

hunted the others. The one who was caught became the next hunter. During the winter, adults played this game mainly to keep warm. Children liked a kind of hide-and-seek in which half of them formed a circle. They covered their eyes or looked at the ground while the others ran and hid. These children signaled when they were all hidden and those in the circle then looked for them. Children also played a game in which they threw spears at a willow hoop rolled on the ground or tossed in the air.

Adults played many games as well, including one similar to soccer. In this game two teams kicked a ball covered with caribou skin, competing to see which team could keep possession of it. In *ajagak*, a cup-and-pin game, people swung a pin made of seal bone on a string. They tried to make the pin stick in each of ten holes (one for each of their fingers) drilled in a row in a large bone. The bone was tied to the other end of the string. They kept count by calling out, "Thumb, one finger, two finger . . ." In a similar game known as *nuglagaqtuq*, a bone with a hole was hung from a string. People tried to thrust a stick in the hole as the bone swung back and forth. The Inuit most often played games when they had gathered together during the long winter months. Other activities, such as cat's cradle, were enjoyed throughout the year. Inuit people made string figures. The figures known as "the two brown bears" and "man carrying a kayak" were popular throughout the Arctic.

4. Beliefs

Inuit beliefs were shaped
by the close relationship
struck between the people
and the land that stretched
for miles around them.

THE INUIT BELIEVED THAT ALL THINGS, LIVING AND NONLIVING, HAD SOULS. They sought to have a respectful relationship with these souls or spirits, especially those of game animals. This was thought to be necessary if people were to maintain health and well-being, because a mistreated animal spirit could become a vengeful monster. People wore sacred amulets and called upon helpful spirits to protect them against evil spirits. Anyone who had suffered misfortune might wander away from the camp for several days and pray to the good spirits for help. The Inuit faced danger not only from the natural world, but from the spirit world as well. As one shaman explained, "We live on a diet of souls."

Their environment, notably the differences between land and sea, also shaped many Inuit practices. They were strictly forbidden to hunt land and sea animals with the same weapons. They also carefully separated food and materials taken from the animals of each realm. Caribou meat had to be cooked on land and sealskins had to be sewn on the sea ice. Meat from sea and land animals could not be stored or cooked together. Caribou meat and freshwater fish, which were considered land creatures, could not be cooked when the Inuit were living on the sea ice, although they could be eaten raw. They could only be cooked on land but not over a fire made from driftwood, which comes from the sea.

The Inuit revered the polar bear because it inhabits both land and water. Because seals and other sea mammals lived in salt water the Inuit believed that they were always thirsty. So, their spirits were soothed if offered a drink of freshwater. It was believed that birds

Inuit deeply respected all animals, not only those they hunted, but their hard-working sled dogs as well.

Both religious ceremonies and social celebrations were accompanied by dancing and drums.

longed for oil, so the Inuit rubbed it on their heads, feet, and wing joints before plucking or skinning them. Spirits of the caribou were deeply offended if Inuit dogs were allowed to gnaw their bones near the place of their death. Wolves and bears were especially dangerous animals and, after a kill, the Inuit made special offerings—a little bow as a gift for a male animal and a strip of hide for a female. It was believed that, like humans, these animals would need these objects for hunting and sewing in the afterlife.

On the day after a kill, the Inuit did not sew out of respect for the animal. When a boy killed his first caribou or seal, his mother wept and ritually wrestled with him over the animal to give the impression that she respectfully mourned its death. The Inuit never mocked game animals or delighted in their pain for fear of being cursed. If they did not observe the proper rituals, the spirits of the air and the sky would be offended. Even the Mother of Sea Mammals, the most powerful spirit, might grow angry and punish them with starvation. The Inuit believed that showing delight during prosperous times might bring ill fortune. So, they tended to be very modest and even complained about their good luck.

People were also respectful of names. When a person died, everyone was forbidden to mention his or her name until a baby received the same name and brought the name back to life. It was believed that the baby would inherit the good traits of the deceased. Similarly, it was considered bad luck to say one's name out loud. Upon arriving at another person's home, visitors simply announced themselves by saying, "Someone is here."

*O*rnately carved, this feather-crested red bear mask is worn by a man during a ceremonial dance.

*T*he Inuit also carved small, intricate wooden masks, which the women placed on their fingers during dances.

It was believed that both male and female shamans were in touch with the supernatural world and able to influence spirits. An individual underwent years of training before being considered a shaman, or *angakok*. Shamans attempted to cure sick people. When a person became seriously ill, the shaman was asked for assistance. The shaman entered into a trance to find the source of the difficulty and the appropriate treatment. By singing, dancing, and beating drums, he or she sought to communicate with the spirits. Occasionally, the spirits appeared to enter the shaman's body, who often rolled on the floor and spoke a strange language. The sick person was comforted that the shaman had at least acted on his or her behalf. Shamans watched over the health of the entire community. When a tragedy befell the group, they tried to ascertain who among them had broken a taboo. Shamans also served as leaders of the community. However, they were feared as much as they were honored. People believed that shamans had so much spiritual power that they could harm anyone who offended them.

Rituals

In sacred rituals, the Inuit appealed to various elements of nature for good weather and successful hunting. Occasionally, they carved revered objects out of wood, bone, and ivory, and adorned them with fur or feathers. They also carved wooden masks that resembled many animals and other spirits in nature. During dances, the men wore masks on their faces, and the women placed miniature masks on their fingers.

Every year, the Inuit had two ceremonies during which they offered thanks for the elements that had helped them to survive. In the Bladder Festival, they sought to liberate the spirits of the whales that had been killed over the past year. Believing the spirits dwelled in the whale bladders, they inflated them with air. After several days of dancing and rituals, they returned the bladders to the sea. The second ceremony was held in the spring. After months of darkness, they dressed in attire that represented both male and female to symbolize creation and welcomed the return of the sun.

European fur traders and missionaries mocked these beliefs and refused to practice them when they came to the Arctic. The Inuit observed that the spirits did not avenge these offenses and began to doubt their own beliefs. As a result, many people abandoned their traditional religion and became Christians. In some cases, the respect for nature was also weakened. People came to believe that wildlife should be dominated and exploited by people, even if the environment was harmed in the process.

Storytelling

Especially during the long, dark winters, the Inuit enjoyed dazzling stories about the sun, the moon, and the seas. These stories were often accompanied by songs, or the storyteller illustrated the tale by drawing pictures in the snow. Many stories dealt with the tension between contrasting or closely related elements—man and woman, land and sea, winter and summer, and dark and light. People not only enjoyed but learned about their way of life through these

Inuit stories often capture the living link between the people and the animals that share their world. Here, a man wears a headpiece that sports a raven's beak.

stories. Among many Inuit, music and storytelling are revered as the highest forms of art.

Stories often concerned survival. The Inuit have kept many of these stories alive by encouraging elders to retell them in schools and even on radio and television programs. Others are writing down the stories so they may not be lost to future generations.

Here is a story from Greenland about the little people who sometimes helped the Inuit survive the severe climate of their homeland.

The Girl Who Married the Little Man

There was once an old couple who had a daughter, and in the village where they lived there were many men who wanted to marry her. The parents, however, wished otherwise and made every effort to keep their daughter at home.

One man in particular was especially eager to make her his wife. He came repeatedly to the house, and at last he fought with the old father and nearly overpowered him. Running swiftly, the old man got to his boat, managed to load it, and narrowly escaped with his wife, daughter, and their belongings.

As they were pulling away, the rejected man and all the other men of the village shouted after them contemptuously, "It won't be easy now for you to get a husband for your daughter. The poor thing can't hunt. How dare you reject us. Just wait until you're hungry, then see if there's anyone to help you."

But the old man kept paddling without bothering to answer, and after a while the family landed on one of the outermost islands. There they built a new house and settled in for the winter.

One morning the old man awoke, saying, "What have I just seen? Was that a man gliding through the doorway?" He questioned his daughter, and as she kept silent he grew suspicious.

When he awoke the next morning he saw the same thing more clearly, a small, stout man slipping out the door. On being questioned, the daughter confessed, "Yes. I am married to one of the little people."

Upon hearing this news, the father did not get upset. His daughter continued, "My husband is afraid you won't like him, so he keeps out of sight. But if you do not mind, he will come live with us."

The next morning, when he opened his eyes, the old man turned toward the entrance and saw nothing unusual. Then, turning around to his daughter's resting place, he saw the little man sitting beneath her lamp.

The father was well pleased and leaned back on his sleeping platform. But when he looked over again, the little man was no longer there.

Toward evening the daughter left the house. When she returned, she had a hunting line, which she hung on a nail to dry. She turned to her parents and told them her husband had come back from hunting and had brought his catch, but now he had gone to take meat to his relatives.

Rushing outside to have a look, the old parents found many freshly killed seals on the beach and rejoiced to see that they were suddenly well supplied with food.

The following morning the old man peeped over the screen that separated him from his daughter's bed, and there was the son-in-law,

Inuit stories also express an abiding faith in the importance of family. Here, two sisters stare out to sea.

seated beneath the lamp as before. In a little while the old man heard someone stirring, and by the time he got up, the son-in-law had already left.

The old man said to his daughter, "Why don't you tell him to spend time with us? We like him very much."

In the evening, when the little man returned with his catch, he stepped inside and made himself at home. The parents were thrilled to have him as a son-in-law, and the family lived happily through the rest of the winter.

When spring came, the son-in-law announced that they would soon be traveling to new hunting grounds for caribou. But first, he said, he would have to visit his own parents. Since he was their only son, he had to provide for them and for his sisters too. So he went to see his family, and when he returned, it was time to start toward the caribou grounds.

The old father put everything into the boat, and when it was loaded and they were ready to set off, another boat suddenly appeared. It was the little man's relatives, come to guide them.

The two boats floated side by side and landed together that evening. The next morning they started out again. When they came in sight of an unfriendly village, the boat full of little people pulled out in front, and their headman called back to the other boat, "Keep close!" All of a sudden the two boats dived down and were paddling beneath the waves. Once past the unfriendly village, they rose back to the surface and safely continued on their way.

Reaching their destination, they made camp for the summer, and the little son-in-law went caribou hunting. When it was time to leave, they piled the boat high with furs and meat. The son-in-law had provided for them plentifully, and on returning to their winter quarters they were comfortable and well off.

Then, news came that the men who had once scorned the old father and his family were now at the point of starvation. Immediately the father set off for the mainland, and before long he returned with all the men who at one time had wished to marry his daughter. They came in a long train of kayaks. When they landed, they were treated hospitably, and the little son-in-law and his wife served them caribou and seal meat.

When the dishes had been set before the guests, the old man said to them in a loud voice, "I wonder if you can still remember what you were telling me a long time ago, when you had nearly killed me, trying to steal my daughter. Can you remember? Your words were these: 'You will surely never get a clever son-in-law.' But in spite of your insults you see what I have. And you said you would never help me if I came to you hungry. Now, please, help yourselves, and eat as much as you like."

5. Changing World

Contact with Europeans brought many changes to the Inuit, including automobiles and, more recently, snowmobiles.

The Thomas Flyer

Put me off at Buffalo

LIVING IN THE FAR NORTH, MOST OF THE INUIT WERE AMONG THE LAST native peoples to come into contact with Europeans. Some Inuit, however, were among the very first. As early as A.D. 984, the Greenland Inuit met a group of Vikings led by Eric the Red. However, another six centuries passed before Martin Frobisher, an English explorer, encountered the Inuit of Greenland and northern Canada in 1576. Frobisher and his party were searching for a water route, known as the Northwest Passage, that would join the Atlantic and Pacific Oceans. Landing on Baffin Island, the Inuit traded peacefully with the English. However, the English kidnapped an Inuit man and took him back to their native country. Frobisher later returned to the Arctic and captured three more Inuit—a man, woman, and child— and brought them to England. Sadly, all the captives died soon after they arrived. Over the years, as Europeans continued to search for the Northwest Passage, they traded metal knives, tools, and guns with the Inuit for fresh meat and fur clothes. The Inuit also acquired goods from the many ships wrecked on the ice.

In 1741, Vitus Bering, a Dane who explored for Russia and for whom the Bering Strait is named, became the first European to encounter the Inuit of Alaska. The region was soon after visited by Russian fur traders. In the late 1700s, Samuel Hearne, who worked for the Hudson's Bay Company, had made contact with the Inuit of northern Canada. The *niovayit*, or traders, supplied Inuit men with steel traps, guns, and ammunition in exchange for a wide variety of hides and furs. In Greenland, the Inuit heaped caribou, polar bear, seal, fox, and hare skins on dogsleds and hauled them to the trading

During his three expeditions to the Arctic between 1576 and 1578, British mariner Martin Frobisher encountered the Inuit.

In the twentieth century, outsiders grew increasingly curious about the Inuit and their way of life. This woman in traditional dress posed for a modern studio portrait, one sign of how greatly her world had changed.

post. In Canada, they trapped beaver, muskrat, mink, fox, wolf, bear, and many other fur-bearing animals sought by the traders. In Alaska, men most often caught seals, beaver, muskrat, mink, and fox, which they traded for sugar, coffee, tea, matches, and other goods.

By the early 1800s, many of the Inuit had begun to abandon their traditional way of life and had become dependent on European goods. They especially sought metal knives and kettles, guns, cloth, and lamps from the Russian, American, and Canadian traders, even though they were often cheated in the exchange. Alcohol was introduced to the Inuit, and it soon had a devastating effect on them.

When the United States acquired Alaska from Russia in 1867, the Americans embarked on many economic ventures, including fur trapping, gold mining, and whaling, that brought them into contact with the Inuit. Despite the flood of settlers, many Inuit groups managed to remain completely isolated from people of European descent until the early 1900s.

The Inuit helped Admiral Robert E. Peary of the United States in his quest to become the first man to reach the North Pole. On April 6, 1909, Peary planted an American flag in the snow at the "Top of the World." Prior to making his famous journey, Peary had studied the Inuit language, habits, and style of dress. He not only won their trust and confidence, but learned to build snow houses and caches for storing food and to drive dog sleds. Four Inuit men—Ootah, Seegloo, Egingwah, and Ooqueah—and his partner Matthew Henson journeyed with Peary. He later said that he never would have reached the North Pole without the assistance of the Inuit.

By 1900, the population of the Inuit had been devastated, due largely to the introduction of diseases for which the Inuit had no immunity. Over the course of the century, the population has climbed back up to earlier levels, with about 117,000 native people living in the sprawling territory.

Inuit Language

Although scattered over thousands of miles of barren tundra and icy coastline, the Inuit all speak similar languages grouped by linguists as Eskimoan. Eskimoan and Aleut, the language of the Aleutian Islands of southwestern Alaska, form the Eskimo-Aleut family. This language family may be distantly related to the Ural-Altaic languages spoken in Finland, Hungary, and Turkey.

The Inuit have numerous words for snow, ice, wind, and other features of their environment. The language that has contributed many words to the English language, such as parka, igloo, kayak, husky, and malamute. The following examples are based on an English-Eskimo dictionary compiled by Arthur Thibert and published in Canada. Most letters are pronounced as in English, with the following exceptions.

k   as in *king*, but occasionally pronounced deep in the throat like *kr* without the *r* being distinctly rolled or spoken. This *k* is noted as *kr* when the alternate pronunciation is required.

j   as *y* in *you*

y   as *y* in *you*

s   as in *ship*, although some groups pronounce it as h (for example, *asso*, meaning *enough* is pronounced *aho*)

i   as in k*ee*n

u   as in sh*oo*t

ng as in si*ng*ing, never as o*ng*oing

dlerk at the end of a sentence is pronounced *tslerk*. Along with *kr*, it is the only really difficult pronunciation.

adult	innark, aktok
antler	nagdjuk
baby	nutaralak
bed	iglerk
berries	paunrait
bird	tingmiark
blubber	orkso
caribou	tuktu
child	nutara, soruserk, krittongak, piarak
chimney	igalerk
coat	koliktar
cold	nigliktok
daughter	panik
dawn	ublarpaluk
daylight	kraumayok
dog	kringmerk
driftwood	tibjak
drum	krilaut
earth	nuna
egg	mannik
fire	ikkuma
fish	irkaluk
floor	natterk

fog	nipterk, tarkserk
food	nerkriksak
frost	patu
frozen meat	koak
fur	amerk mitkrolik
girl, young	niviasar
gloves	adgauyait, poalu
grandchild	erngutak, ernrutak
guest	tuyurmiangoyok
guide	krauyimatauyok
harpoon (spear)	nauligak, unark, kapût
home	aisimabvik, ainiarvik
house	iglu
husband	ui
ice	sikku, koasak
iceberg	pikaluyak
island	kekertak
land	nuna
man	inuk
marriage	nulliarengnerk
meat	nerkri
melting ice (for water)	immiugak
midnight	unnuar kretirarlugo
mitten	poalu

moon	tatkret
moon, full	tatkresiwok
morning	ublar
moss	manerk
night	unnuar
north	kannernark
polar bear	nanuk
sea	tareor
seal	netjerk, netserk
sky	krilak
sled	kamotik, kramotik
snow (first snowfall)	apingaut
son	ernerk
star	ublureak
summer	auyark, auyak
sun	sikrinerk
teacher	ajokertuye, illiniartitsiye
village	iglurdjuartalik
walrus	aiverk
water	immerk
weather	sila
whale blubber	orksok
wife	nilliak
woman	arnak

6. New Ways

No longer an isolated people, the next generation of Inuit faces the changes brought by the twenty-first century.

THE INUIT THROUGHOUT THE ARCTIC HAVE STRUGGLED TO UPHOLD THEIR traditional way of life. Oil drilling, mining, and large-scale commercial fishing and whaling, along with military activities in the far north, have drastically reduced the populations of land and sea animals. Many Inuit have also adopted European tools, including metal guns and knives. Women have acquired sewing machines, and men have purchased snowmobiles and motorboats. Many people have moved into permanent wood-frame houses, which has made their old ways of seasonal migration seem impractical and out-of-date. Yet many of these homes do not have running water. Every week, a water truck comes and fills a tank in each home.

In recent years, many Inuit have continued to adopt a more modern way of life, including the use of computers and other technology. Many people have taken jobs, shop at supermarkets, and live in carpenter-built homes. The Inuit in Greenland have been especially influenced by Danish culture, while the people of Siberia have been affected by the political changes of the former Soviet Union and now Russia. Instead of families providing for themselves, many Inuit in Siberia now hunt seals, walrus, and whales as part of a group known as a collective. In other regions, some Inuit groups have begun to herd reindeer or cattle and grow crops hardy enough to survive the brief, chilly summers.

In Alaska, the Inuit remained isolated until the mid-1900s when the U.S. government began to provide them with basic schools and medical services. The discovery of gas and oil, as well as the surge in mining operations, have brought dramatic changes. American

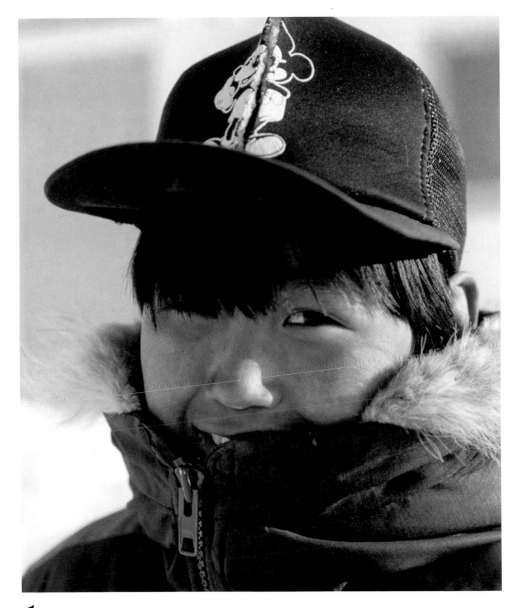

*I*nuit children are often raised to be citizens of the modern world without neglecting their traditional ways.

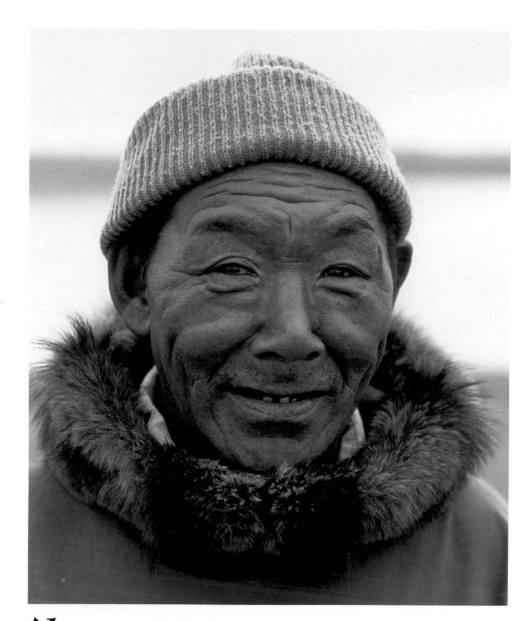

*N*ever succumbing to the unforgiving conditions of their world, for generations the Inuit have thrived in some of Earth's harshest terrain.

workers poured into the region, and many Inuit took jobs on the construction projects. Similarly, because of oil and mineral exploitation, the Inuit of Canada have also come into much greater contact with the outside world in recent years. Many Alaska Inuit have left their small communities and moved to cities. Today, nearly half live in urban areas, away from their friends and families.

In 1971, the Alaska Inuit received $962 million and 44 million acres of land in exchange for giving up their claim to 335 million acres. Known as the Alaska Native Claims Settlement Act (ANCSA), this agreement was reached largely because the U.S. government planned to permit construction of the Trans-Alaska Pipeline across Inuit territory. In this agreement, the Inuit and other native peoples gained legal ownership of 12 percent of Alaska and received funds desperately needed for economic development. Many Inuit villages in Alaska have formed corporations to more effectively represent their interests. In 1980, the U.S. government amended ANCSA with the Alaska National Interest Lands Conservation Act (ANILCA). This measure restored rights of native peoples to hunt and fish their lands and water.

In Canada, the Inuit movement for self-determination began in 1974. Three years later, in 1977, a native organization called Inuit Tapirisat of Canada (ITC) put forth a proposal to create a new province to be known as Nunavat. The proposal was again advanced in 1979. In 1982, eighty-five percent of voters in the eastern Arctic region of Canada decided in favor of establishing a new province from the eastern and northern parts of the Northwest Territories to be known as Nunavut, which means "our land." On December 16, 1991, the Canadian government granted the Inuit the right to govern this new territory of 770,000 square miles, an area larger than the states of Alaska and Texas combined. They were also awarded $1.14 billion in exchange for relinquishing all other land claims in Canada. The agreement went into effect in 1999.

Today, the Inuit are struggling to maintain their traditional ways at the distant edges of a modern world. With less game and fish, along with limits on hunting endangered animals, people have greater difficulty providing for themselves. They must now purchase much of their food and household goods. Yet, transporting groceries and goods over long distances by plane, truck, or boat is expensive, so people must pay high prices. With few jobs in villages, many people leave their homes and families to work at seasonal jobs in mills, mines, or fish-processing plants. In recent years, many Inuit have sought employment with oil companies.

Many parents encourage their children to study hard in school and to attend college to become teachers, engineers, business managers, doctors, and lawyers. Although more schools are being constructed, many young people must still leave home to attend high school. They miss their families, yet many people believe that this is the only way they will have a chance for a prosperous life. Many Inuit also use the radio and the Internet to communicate among far-flung settlements, as well as for education and social services. At the same time, however, the Inuit do not wish their children to lose touch with their heritage. Older people often come to school to share traditional stories and show children how to sew and make fish traps. Men still teach their sons how to hunt seals and how to survive winter storms. They want their children to know that they can make a living and love the land of their ancestors.

More About

the Innit

Time Line

between 3,000 and 1,000 B.C. Inuit migrate on foot and by dogsled from Siberia to North America across the Bering Strait long after other peoples had come to the continent. Some scholars believe the time of migration may have been earlier, between 6,000 and 5,000 B.C.

984 Led by Eric the Red, the Vikings makes contact with the Inuit of Greenland.

1576 Martin Frobisher, an English explorer, encounters the Central Inuit of northern Canada.

1741 Vitus Bering, an explorer for Russia, is the first European to make contact with the Inuit of Alaska.

1867 The United States acquires Alaska from Russia.

1900 The Inuit population is devastated by diseases.

1909 With help of the Inuit, Admiral Robert E. Peary and Matthew Henson of the United States reach the North Pole on April 6.

1971 In the Alaska Native Claims Settlement Act (ANCSA) the Inuit of Alaska receive $962 million and 44 million acres of land in exchange for giving up claims to 335 million acres.

1982 Canada forms a new province from the eastern and northern parts of the Northwest Territories to be known as Nunavut, meaning "our land."

1999 The Canadian government agrees to give control of Nunavut, encompassing one-fifth of the total land area of Canada, to the Inuit.

Notable People

William L. Hensley (1941–   ), also known as Iggiagruk which means Big Hill or Little Mountain, has served as a native leader in Alaska since he graduated from George Washington University in 1966. While studying in Washington, D.C., he wondered why his people, who lived in poverty, were not represented in Congress. He became one of the founders of the Alaska Federation of Natives (AFN), an organization that represents many villages and a number of social service organizations. With Hensley serving in several key positions, the AFN successfully lobbied Congress to pass the Alaska Native Claims Settlement Act of 1971, legislation that granted nearly $1 billion and 44 million acres of land to Alaskan natives.

William L. Hensley

In 1968, Hensley was appointed to serve on the National Council on Indian Opportunity. He also received the John F. Kennedy Memorial Award, the National Public Service Award from the Rockefeller Foundation, and many other honors. He was elected to the Alaska House of Representatives for two terms, serving from 1967 to 1971 before serving as a senator from 1970 to 1974. Hensley again served as senator in 1986. Over the years, he has remained active in public service, including programs in education, suicide prevention, and alcohol abuse.

He has also been actively involved with wildlife management and the hunting and fishing rights of Alaskan natives.

Kenojuak (1927–   ), artist, was born on Baffin Island, Northwest Territories, Canada. The daughter of Ushuakjuk, a hunter and trader, and his wife Seelaki, Kenojuak was named after her deceased maternal grandfather. When her father was murdered in a dispute in their camp in 1933, Kenojuak went to live with her grandmother, Koweesa, who taught her sewing.

When Kenojuak was nineteen, her mother and stepfather, Takpaugni, arranged for her to marry a hunter named Johnniebo. A spirited young woman, she threw rocks at her husband, but came to love him as a kind and gentle man. In the early years of her marriage, she gave birth to two daughters who died of food poisoning and a son who was adopted by another family at birth. Adoption was a common Inuit custom. In 1950, the first nurse arrived in the north to offer medical care. Kenojuak was diagnosed with tuberculosis and sent to Parc Savard Hospital in Quebec City, where she was treated from 1952 to 1955. During this time, she made dolls and did beadwork.

When she returned to her family in the north, Kenojuak began to devote herself to her art, notably sealskin and beaded crafts. She also began carving and drawing. With the encouragement of James Houston, an early supporter of Inuit art, she persevered and in 1958 her first print, *Rabbit Eating Seaweed*, was made from a design on one of her sealskin bags. With Houston's help, Kenojuak and several other Inuit of Cape Dorset formed the West Baffin Eskimo Cooperative in 1959. The group served as a *senlavik*, or "place where one works." Several of Kenojuak's drawings were displayed and favorably reviewed. In 1962, the National Film Board of Canada made a documentary about her life entitled *Eskimo Artist—Kenojuak* that brought considerable public attention to her work.

In 1967, Kenojuak received the Order of Canada Medal of Service, and her work was featured in the National Gallery of Canada. She became

Kenojuak

especially well-known for the vivid colors and intricate design of her drawings of birds and people. Three years later, one of her most famous works, *The Enchanted Owl*, appeared on a six-cent Canadian postage stamp. In 1972, she was honored with membership in the Royal Canadian Academy, and over the years her work had been widely exhibited in Canada, the United States and Europe. In 1986, a thirty-year retrospective of her work was exhibited at the McMichael Canadian Collection Gallery in Kleinsburg, Ontario, just outside Toronto. Although she is best known for her drawings and paintings, she also carves and sculpts soapstone. Despite her widespread fame, Kenojuak continues to work within the culture of the Inuit people. With her third husband, Joanassie Igiu, and her six children, she enjoys the outdoors and often fishes and hunts at favorite campsites. She once said, "The main reason why I create things is because of my children, my family."

Howard Rock (1911–1976), editor and publisher, was born in Point Hope, Alaska. As a young man, he attended St. Thomas Mission and later worked his way to the Pacific Northwest where he studied art at the University of Washington in Seattle. He became a jewelry designer. During World War II, he served in the U.S. Army Air Force in North Africa. After the war, Rock returned to Alaska where he became active in public service. Recognizing the need for a native newspaper, he sought financial support and established the *Tundra Times* in 1962. Serving as publisher and editor, he became highly regarded for his strong advocacy of the rights of Alaska natives. A year before his death, he was nominated for a Pulitzer Prize.

Glossary

aglu A breathing hole in the ice used by seals

amaut A parka hood in which a baby was kept warm

amulet A small sacred object believed to provide protection and bring good fortune

angakok A shaman with powers for healing the body and spirit

blubber Fat from a whale or other sea mammal, often eaten as food and melted or oil for lamps

cache A hiding place for food and belongings

igloo An Inuit house made of snow, skin, or other materials

inua A spirit or soul, especially of a game animal

kamiks Insulated shoes made of animals skins; also called mukluks

kayak A slender, pointed canoe sheathed with animals skins, with a hole on top in which the paddler sits

karmat A square or rectangular house built by Inuit, especially by those living in Greenland and Alaska

kashim A large building used by men for ceremonies

kudlik A lamp used to warm a home and dry clothing

mukluks Warm shoes made of animals skins; also called kamiks

muktuk The layer of fat under a whale's skin

niovayit A trader

nuglagaqtuq A popular Inuit game

sea ice Ice that forms on the ocean as a solid sheet or as ice floes

sinew Tough animal tissue joining muscle to bone and used by the Inuit as thread

taboo A required or forbidden practice that ensures health and well-being

throat singing A type of singing within the throat that makes a deep, nasal sound

tundra Low, treeless land of the north that becomes marshy in the warm months, but never thaws beneath the surface

ulu A curved knife

umiak An open boat covered in animals skins in which several people hunt or travel together

Further Information

The story entitled "The Creation" is adapted from *The Mackenzie Eskimos: After Knud Rasmussen's Posthumous Notes* published by Gyldendal, Copenhagen, in 1942 and reprinted by AMS Press, New York, in 1976.

"The Girl Who Married the Little Man" adapted by John Bierhorst is reprinted with permission from *The Deetkatoo: Native American Stories about Little People* published by William Morrow and Company, New York, 1998.

Birket-Smith, Kaj. *The Caribou Eskimos: Material and Social Life and Their Cultural Position.* Washington, D.C.: Brookhaven Press, 1978.

Boas, Franz. "The Central Eskimo." *Sixth Annual Report of the Bureau of American Ethnology, 1884–1885.* Washington, D.C.: Smithsonian Institution, Bureau of American Ethnology, 1888. Pp. 399-669.

Burch, Ernest S., and Werner Forman. *The Eskimos.* Norman. University of Oklahoma Press, 1988.

Condon, Richard G., and Julia Ogina. *The Northern Copper Inuit: A History.* Norman: University of Oklahoma Press, 1996.

Crandall, Richard C. *Inuit Art: A History.* Jefferson, NC: McFarland, 2000.

Dumond, Don E. *The Eskimos and Aleuts.* New York: Thames and Hudson, 1987.

Eber, Dorothy. *When the Whalers Were Up North: Inuit Memories from the Eastern Arctic.* Norman: University of Oklahoma Press, 1996.

The Encyclopedia of North American Indians. New York: Marshall Cavendish, 1997.

Hessel, Ingo, and Dieter Hessel. *Inuit Art: An Introduction.* New York: Harry N. Abrams, 1998.

The Inuit of Canada. Hull, Quebec: Publications and Public Enquiries, Department of Indian Affairs and Development, 1995.

Johansen, Bruce E., and Donald A. Grinde. *The Encyclopedia of Native American Biography*. New York: Henry Holt and Co., 1997.

King, J. C. H. *Arctic Hunters: Indians and Inuit of Northern Canada*. London: Published for the Trustees of British Museum by British Museum Publications in association with Indigenous Survival International, 1987.

Lowenstein, Tom. *Ancient Land, Sacred Whale: The Inuit Hunt and Its Rituals*. New York: Farrar, Straus, and Giroux, 1994.

MacDonald, John. *The Arctic Sky: Inuit Astronomy, Star Lore, and Legend*. Toronto: Royal Ontario Museum/Nunavut Research Institute, 1998.

Malinowski, Sharon, and Anna Sheets. *The Gale Encyclopedia of Native American Tribes*. Detroit: Gale Research, 1998.

Malinowski, Sharon. *Notable Native Americans*. Detroit: Gale Research, 1995.

Mathiassen, Therkel. *Material Culture of the Iglulik Eskimos*. Washington, D.C.: Brookhaven Press, 1978.

Morrison, David A. *Inuit: Glimpses of an Arctic Past*. Hull, Québec: Canadian Museum of Civilization, 1995.

Nansen, Fridtjof. *Eskimo Life*. New York: AMS Press, 1975.

Nungak, Zebedee, and Eugene Arima. *Inuit Stories: Povungnituk*. Hull, Québec: Canadian Museum of Civilization, National Museums of Canada, 1988.

Rasmussen, Knud. *Intellectual Culture of the Copper Eskimos*. Washington, D.C.: Brookhaven Press, 1978.

Rasmussen, Knud. *Knud Rasmussen's Posthumous Notes on East Greenland Legends and Myths*. New York: AMS Press, 1976, 1939.

———. *The People of the Polar North: A Record*. New York: AMS Press, 1976, 1908.

Rink, H. *Tales and Traditions of the Eskimo, With a Sketch of Their Habits, Religion, Language and Other Peculiarities*. New York: AMS Press, 1975.

Siska, Heather Smith. *The Haida and the Inuit: People of the Seasons*. Vancouver, BC: Douglas & McIntyre, 1984.

Steltzer, Ulli. *Inuit: The North in Transition*. Seattle: University of Washington Press, 1982.

Sturtevant, William C., and David Damas. *Handbook of North American Indians.*

Volume 5. Arctic. Washington, D.C.: Smithsonian Institution, 1984.

Sutton, George Miksch. *Eskimo Year*. Norman: University of Oklahoma Press, 1985.

Taylor, J. Garth. *The Canadian Eskimos*. Toronto: Royal Ontario Museum, 1971.

Thibert, Arthur. *Dictionary: English-Eskimo, Eskimo-English*. Ottawa: Research Centre for Amerindian Anthropology, University of Ottawa, 1954.

Wright, J. V. *A History of the Native People of Canada*. Hull, Quebec: Canadian Museum of Civilization, 1995.

Children's Books

Bierhorst, John. *The Dancing Fox: Arctic Folktales*. New York: Morrow, 1997.

Bonvillain, Nancy. *The Inuit*. New York: Chelsea House Publishers, 1995.

Cordoba, Yasmine A. *Igloo*. Vero Beach, FL: Rourke, 2001.

Dabcovich, Lydia. *The Polar Bear Son: An Inuit Tale*. New York: Clarion Books, 1997.

Finley, Carol. *Art of the Far North: Inuit Sculpture, Drawing, and Printmaking*. Minneapolis: Lerner, 1998.

Fleischner, Jennifer. *The Inuits: People of the Arctic*. Brookfield, CT: Millbrook Press, 1995.

Hancock, Lyn. *Nunavut*. Minneapolis: Lerner Publications, 1995.

Kusugak, Michael, and Vladyana Krykorka. *Arctic Stories*. Toronto: Annick Press, 1998.

Lassieur, Allison. *The Inuit*. Mankato, MN: Bridgestone Books, 2000.

Newman, Shirlee Petkin. *The Inuits*. New York: Franklin Watts, 1993.

Pelly, David F. *Inuit of the North*. Toronto: Grolier, 1988.

Shemie, Bonnie. *Houses of Snow, Skin and Bones: Native Dwellings, the Far North*. Montreal: Tundra Books, 1989.

Smith, J. H. Greg. *Eskimos: The Inuit of the Arctic*. Vero Beach, FL: Rourke, 1987.

Websites

Arctic National Wildlife Refuge

http://www.r7.fws.gov/nwr/arctic/arctic.html

Inuit Art Foundation

http://www.inuitart.org/

Inuit Culture

http://www.arctictravel.com/chapters/incultpage.html

Inuktitut–The Language of the Inuit People

http://www.arctic.ca/LUS/Inuktitut.html

Iñupiat of Arctic Alaska

http://arcticcircle.uconn.edu/HistoryCulture/Inupiat/

Inuuqatigiit: The Curriculum from the Inuit Perspective

http://siksik.learnnet.nt.ca/Inuuqatigiit/1/index.htm

The Inuvialuit of the Western Arctic

http://www.civilization.ca/membrs/fph/inuvial/indexe.html

The Native Peoples of Alaska and their Eskimo Culture

http://www.alaska.net/~nome/eculture.htm

North: Landscape of the Imagination

http://www.nlc-bnc.ca/north/norint-e.htm

Nunavut Tunngavik Incorporated

http://www.tunngavik.com/

Satuumavik School, Kangiqsualujjuaq (Quebec)

http://www3.sympatico.ca/satuumavik/Eng/index.html

Index

Page numbers in **boldface** are illustrations.

Raymond Bial

HAS PUBLISHED MORE THAN THIRTY CRITICALLY ACCLAIMED BOOKS OF PHO-tographs for children and adults. His photo-essays for children include *Corn Belt Harvest, Amish Home, Frontier Home, Shaker Home, The Underground Railroad, Portrait of a Farm Family, With Needle and Thread: A Book About Quilts, Mist Over the Mountains: Appalachia and Its People, Cajun Home,* and *Where Lincoln Walked.*

He is currently immersed in writing *Lifeways*, a series of books about Native Americans. As with his other work, Bial's deep feeling for his subjects is evident in both the text and illustrations. He travels to tribal cultural centers, photographing homes, artifacts, and sur-roundings and learning firsthand about the national lifeways of these peoples.

A librarian at a small college in Champaign, Illinois, he lives with his wife and three children in nearby Urbana.